TAGALOG

(PILIPINO)

Made Nice & Easy!®

Staff of Research & Education Association
Carl Fuchs, Language Program Director

Based on Language Courses developed by the
U.S. Government for Foreign Service Personnel

Research & Education Association
Visit our website at
www.rea.com

Research & Education Association
61 Ethel Road West
Piscataway, New Jersey 08854
E-mail: info@rea.com

TAGALOG MADE NICE & EASY®

Year 2007 Printing

Printed in the United States of America

Library of Congress Control Number 00-193034

International Standard Book Number 0-87891-378-5

What This Guide Will Do For You

Whether travelling to a foreign country or to your favorite international restaurant, this *Nice & Easy* guide gives you just enough of the language to get around and be understood. Much of the material in this book was developed for government personnel who are often assigned to a foreign country on a moment's notice and need a quick introduction to the language.

In this handy and compact guide, you will find useful words and phrases, popular expressions, common greetings, and the words for numbers, money, and time. Every word or phrase is accompanied with the correct pronunciation and spelling. There is a vocabulary list for finding words quickly.

Generous margins on the pages allow you to make notes and remarks that you may find helpful.

If you expect to travel to the Philippines, the section on the country's history and relevant up-to-date facts will make your trip more informative and enjoyable. By keeping this guide with you, you'll be well prepared to understand as well as converse in Tagalog.

Carl Fuchs
Language Program Director

Contents

PHILIPPINES

FACTS & HISTORY

Official Name: Republic of the Philippines

Geography
Area: 300,000 sq. km. (117,187 sq. mi.).
Cities: *Capital* - Manila (pop. 9.9 million in metropolitan area); Davao (1.2 million), Cebu (0.7 million).
Terrain: Islands, 65% mountainous, with narrow coastal lowlands.
Climate: Tropical, astride typhoon belt.

People
Nationality: *Noun* - Filipino(s). *Adjective* - Philippine.
Population: 83.9 million.
Annual growth rate: 2.36%.
Ethnic groups: Malay, Chinese.
Religions: Catholic 85%, Protestant 9%, Muslim 5%, Buddhist and other 1%.
Languages: Pilipino (based on Tagalog), national language; English, language of government and instruction in higher education.

Government
Type: Republic.
Independence: 1946.
Constitution: February 11, 1987.
Branches: *Executive* - president and vice president. *Legislative* - bicameral legislature. *Judicial* - independent.

Economy
GDP: $84.2 billion.
GDP per capita: $976.
Annual growth rate: 6.1%.
Natural resources: Copper, nickel, iron, cobalt, silver, gold.
Agriculture: *Products* - sugar, coconut products, rice, corn, pork, pineapple products, bananas, aquaculture, mangoes, eggs.
Industry: *Types* - textiles and garments, pharmaceuticals, chemicals, wood products, food processing, electronics assembly, petroleum refining, fishing.
Trade (2004): *Exports* - $39.6 billion. *Imports* - $40.3 billion.

People and Language

The majority of Philippine people are descendants of Indonesians and Malays who migrated to the islands long before the Christian era. The most significant ethnic minority group is the Chinese, who have played an important role in commerce since the ninth century when they first came to the islands to trade. As a result of intermarriage, many Filipinos have some Chinese and Spanish ancestry. Americans and Spaniards constitute the next largest alien minorities in the country. About 90% of the people are Christian; most were converted and Westernized to varying degrees during nearly 400 years of Spanish and American rule. The major non-Hispanicized groups are the Muslim population, concentrated in the Sulu Archipelago and in central and western Mindanao, and the mountain groups of northern Luzon. Small forest tribes live in the more remote areas of Mindanao.

About 87 native languages and dialects are spoken, all belonging to the Malay-Polynesian linguistic family. Of these, eight are the first languages of more than 85% of the population. The three principal indigenous languages are Cebuano, spoken in the Visayas; Tagalog, predominant in the area around Manila; and Ilocano, spoken in northern Luzon. Since 1939, in an effort to develop national unity, the government has promoted the use of the national language, Pilipino, which is based on Tagalog. Pilipino is taught in all schools and is gaining acceptance, particularly as a second language. English, the most important nonnative language, is used as a second language by many, including nearly all professionals, academics, and government workers. In 2003, the president ordered the Department of Education to restore English as the medium of instruction in all schools and universities. Only a few Filipino families retain Spanish usage. Despite this multiplicity of languages, the Philippines has one of the highest literacy rates in the East Asian and Pacific area. About 92% of the population 10 years of age and older are literate.

History

The history of the Philippines may be divided into four distinct phases: the pre-Spanish period (before 1521); the Spanish period (1521-1898); the American period (1898-1946); and the years since independence (1946-present).

Pre-Spanish Period

The first people in the Philippines, the Negritos, are believed to have come to the islands 30,000 years ago from Borneo and Sumatra, making their way across then-existing land bridges. Subsequently, people of Malay descent came from the south in successive waves, the earliest by land bridges and later in boats called barangays. The Malays settled in scattered communities, also called barangays, which were ruled by chieftains known as datus. Chinese merchants and traders arrived and settled in the ninth century A.D. In the 14th century, Arabs arrived, introducing Islam in the south and extending some influence even into Luzon. The Malays, however, remained the dominant group until the Spanish arrived in the 16th century.

Spanish Period

Ferdinand Magellan claimed the Philippines for Spain in 1521, and for the next 377 years, the islands were under Spanish rule. This period was the era of conversion to Roman Catholicism. A Spanish colonial social system was developed, complete with a strong centralized government and considerable clerical influence. The Filipinos were restive under the Spanish, and this long period was marked by numerous uprisings. The most important of these began in 1896 under the leadership of Emilio Aguinaldo and continued until the Americans defeated the Spanish fleet in Manila Bay on May 1, 1898, during the Spanish-American War. Aguinaldo declared independence from Spain on June 12, 1898.

American Period

Following Admiral Dewey's defeat of the Spanish fleet in Manila Bay, the United States occupied the Philippines. Spain ceded the islands to the United States under the terms of the Treaty of Paris (December 10, 1898) that ended the war. A war of resistance against U.S. rule, led by revolutionary President Aguinaldo, broke out in 1899. Although Americans have historically used the term "the Philippine Insurrection," Filipinos and an increasing number of American historians refer to these hostilities as the Philippine-American War (1899-1902), and in 1999 the U.S. Library of Congress reclassified its references to use this term. In 1901, Aguinaldo was captured and swore allegiance to the United States, and resistance gradually died out. U.S. administration of the Philippines was always declared to be temporary and aimed to develop institutions that would permit and encourage the eventual establishment of a free and democratic government. Therefore, U.S. officials concentrated on the creation of such practical supports for democratic government as public education and a sound legal system.

The first legislative assembly was elected in 1907. A bicameral legislature, largely under Philippine control, was established. A civil service was formed and was gradually taken over by the Filipinos, who had effectively gained control by the end of World War I. The Catholic Church was disestablished, and a considerable amount of church land was purchased and redistributed. In 1935, under the terms of the Tydings-McDuffie Act, the Philippines became a self-governing commonwealth. Manuel Quezon was elected president of the new government, which was designed to prepare the country for independence after a 10-year transition period. World War II intervened, however, and in May 1942, Corregidor, the last American/Filipino stronghold, fell. U.S. forces in the Philippines surrendered to the Japanese, placing the islands under Japanese control.

The war to regain the Philippines began when Gen. Douglas MacArthur landed on Leyte on October 20, 1944. Filipinos and Americans fought together until the Japanese surrender in September 1945. Much of Manila was destroyed during the final months of the fighting, and an estimated one million Filipinos lost their lives in the war. As a result of the Japanese occupation, the guerrilla warfare that followed, and the battles leading to liberation, the country suffered great damage and a complete organizational breakdown. Despite the shaken state of the country, the United States and the Philippines decided to move forward with plans for independence. On July 4, 1946, the Philippine Islands became the independent Republic of the Philippines, in accordance with the terms of the Tydings-McDuffie Act. In 1962, the official Independence Day was changed from July 4 to June 12, commemorating the date that independence from Spain was declared by General Aguinaldo in 1898.

Post-Independence Period

The early years of independence were dominated by U.S.-assisted postwar reconstruction. A communist-inspired Huk Rebellion (1945-53) complicated recovery efforts before its successful suppression under the leadership of President Ramon Magsaysay. The succeeding administrations of Presidents Carlos P. Garcia (1957-61) and Diosdado Macapagal (1961-65) sought to expand Philippine ties to their Asian neighbors, implement domestic reform programs, and develop and diversify the economy.

In 1972, President Ferdinand E. Marcos (1965-86) declared martial law, citing growing lawlessness and open rebellion by the communist rebels as his justification. Marcos governed from 1973 until mid-1981 in accordance with the transitory provisions of a new constitution that replaced the commonwealth constitution of 1935. He suppressed democratic institutions and restricted civil liberties during the martial law period, ruling largely by decree and popular referenda. The government began a process of political normalization during 1978-81, culminating in the reelection of President Marcos to a 6-year term that would have ended in 1987. The Marcos government's respect for human rights remained low despite the end of martial law on January 17, 1981. His government retained its wide arrest and detention powers. Corruption and favoritism contributed to a serious decline in economic growth and development under Marcos.

The assassination of opposition leader Benigno (Ninoy) Aquino upon his return to the Philippines in 1983, after a long period of exile, coalesced popular dissatisfaction with Marcos and set in motion a succession of events that culminated in a snap presidential election in February 1986. The opposition united under Aquino's widow, Corazon Aquino, and Salvador Laurel, head of the United Nationalist Democratic Organization (UNIDO). The election was marred by widespread electoral fraud on the part of Marcos and his supporters. International observers, including a U.S. delegation led by Sen. Richard Lugar (R-Indiana), denounced the official results. Marcos was forced to flee the Philippines in the face of a peaceful civilian-military uprising that ousted him and installed Corazon Aquino as president on February 25, 1986.

Under Aquino's presidency progress was made in revitalizing democratic institutions and respect for civil liberties. However, the administration was also viewed by many as weak and fractious, and a return to full political stability and economic development was hampered by several attempted coups staged by disaffected members of the Philippine military.

Fidel Ramos was elected president in 1992. Early in his administration, Ramos declared "national reconciliation" his highest priority. He legalized the Communist Party and created the National Unification Commission (NUC) to lay the groundwork for talks with communist insurgents, Muslim separatists, and military rebels. In June 1994, President Ramos signed into law a general conditional amnesty covering all rebel groups, as well as Philippine military and police personnel accused of crimes committed while fighting the insurgents.

The election in May 1998 of popular movie actor Joseph Ejercito Estrada as president marked the Philippines' third democratic succession since the ouster of Marcos. Gloria Macapagal-Arroyo, elected vice president in 1998, assumed the presidency in January 2001 after widespread demonstrations that followed the breakdown of Estrada's impeachment trial on corruption charges. National and local elections took place in May 2004. Under the constitution, Macapagal-Arroyo was eligible for another six-year term as president, and she won a hard-fought campaign against her primary challenger.

Economy

Since the end of the Second World War, the Philippine economy has had a mixed history of growth and development. Over the years, the Philippines has gone from being one of the richest countries in Asia (following

Japan) to being one of the poorest. Growth immediately after the war was rapid, but slowed over time. A severe recession in 1984-85 saw the economy shrink by more than 10%, and perceptions of political instability during the Aquino administration further dampened economic activity. During his administration, President Ramos introduced a broad range of economic reforms and initiatives designed to spur business growth and foreign investment. As a result, the Philippines saw a period of rapid sustained growth, but the spreading Asian financial crisis has slowed economic development in the Philippines once again.

The Philippines was less severely affected by the Asian financial crisis than its neighbors, due in considerable part to remittances of approximately $5 billion annually from overseas workers. Nonetheless, the country continues to be a weak economic performer. The Philippines relies heavily on electronics shipments for about two-thirds of export revenues. Although there has been some improvement over the years, local value added of electronics exports remains relatively low, at about 30%.

The Philippine economy juggles extremely limited financial resources while attempting to meet the needs of a rapidly expanding population and address intensifying demands for the current administration to deliver on its anti-poverty promises. Over 80% of the government budget is gobbled up by non-discretionary expenses (i.e., debt service, government salaries and benefits, and legally mandated revenue transfers to local government units). The current high level of government debt, the substantial share of foreign obligations, the emerging risks posed by contingent liabilities, and the worrisome deterioration in the tax collection performance from the 1997 peak (still low by regional standards) have increased the country's vulnerability to severe external and domestic shocks. More recent reforms include laws increasing excise taxes on tobacco and liquor products and establishing a system of rewards and penalties in revenue collection agencies.

Potential foreign investors, as well as tourists, continue to be concerned about law and order, inadequate infrastructure, and governance issues. While trade liberalization presents significant opportunities, intensifying global competition and the emergence of low-wage export economies also pose challenges. Competition from other Southeast Asian countries and from China for investment underlines the need for sustained progress on structural reforms to remove bottlenecks to growth, lower costs of doing business, and promote good public and private sector governance. The government has been working to reinvigorate its anti-corruption drive and the Office of the Ombudsman has reported improved conviction rates. Nevertheless, the Philippines will need to do more to improve international perception of its anti-corruption campaign—an effort that will require strong political will and significantly greater financial and human resources.

The Philippines

CHINA

TAIWAN

PHILIPPINES

MALAYSIA

LUZON

MANILA

PACIFIC
OCEAN

MINDORO

SOUTH
CHINA SEA

SAMAR

ILOILO

LEYTE

CEBU

BOHOL

NEGROS

PALAWAN

SULU SEA

MINDANAO

ZAMBOANGA

2

4

Hints on Pronunciation

All the words and phrases are written in a spelling which you read like English. Each letter or combination of letters is used for the sound it normally represents in English and it *always* stands for the same sound. Thus, "oo" is always pronounced as in *too, boot, tooth, roost,* never as in *blood* or *door.* Say these words and then pronounce the vowel sound by itself. That is the sound you must use every time you see "oo" in the Pronunciation column. If you should use some other sound—for example, the one in *blood* or the one in *door*—you might be misunderstood.

Syllables that are accented — that is, pronounced louder than others — are written in capital letters. Curved lines (‿) are used to show sounds that are pronounced together without any break; for example "S‿YAHM" meaning "nine."

Special Points

AY
as in *day, may, say,* but cut short. Example: "kar-NAY" meaning "meat."

O *or* OA
as in *go, boat, load* but cut short. Example: "ah-NO" meaning "what," "ka-HA-poan" meaning "yesterday."

OW	as in *how, now, town*. Example: "na-oo-OO-how" meaning "thirsty."
(')	follows vowels which are cut off sharply at the end. Examples: "sahm-POO'" meaning "ten," "PO'" meaning "sir" or "madam," "heen-DEE'" meaning "no," "ah-LEE-la'" meaning "servant."
NG	stands for the *ng*-sound we have in *sing, bring, ring*. In English it comes only at the end of words, but in Tagalog it also comes at the beginning. Example: "nga-YOAN" meaning "today."
G	always stands for the sound we have in *get, give, go*, never for the sound in *gem, George, gee*. Example: "geen-o-OANG" meaning "Mr."

USEFUL WORDS AND PHRASES

GREETINGS AND GENERAL PHRASES

English	*Pronunciation*	*Tagalog Spelling*
Good morning	ma-gahn-DAHNG oo-MA-ga PO'	Magandang umaga pô
Good afternoon	ma-gahn-DAHNG HA-poan PO'	Magandang hapon pô

English	Pronunciation	Tagalog Spelling
Good evening	ma-gahn-DAHNG ga-BEE PO'	Magandang gabí pô

The word "PO'" in the last three expressions is a general term of respect used when speaking to both men and women. Listen to the word again and repeat: "PO', PO'." Notice that the sound of the vowel is cut off very sharply, the way some people do when they say "No'." All vowels which end like this are written with an apostrophe after them. Try the word again: "PO', PO'."

Mr. Santos	geen-o-OANG SAHN-toass	Ginoong Santos
Mrs. Santos	GEEN-ahng SAHN-toass	Ginang Santos
Miss Santos	bee-nee-BEE-neeng SAHN-toass	Binibining Santos
How are you?	ka-moo-sta PO' ka-YO?	Kamusta pô kayo?
Fine	ma-BOO-tay po'	Mabute pô
Please	pa-kee-SOO-yo'	Pakisuyò

12

English	Pronunciation	Tagalog Spelling
Thank you	sa-LA-maht po'	Salamat pô
You're welcome	wa-LA' poang ah-no-MAHN	Walâ pong anoman
Excuse me	pa-TA-wahd po'	Pataward pô
Yes	O-po'	Opô
No	heen-DEE' po'	Hindî pô
Do you understand?	na ee-een-teen-dee-HAHN ba NEEN-yo?	Na iintindihan ba ninyo?
I don't understand	heen-DEE' ko po' na ee-een-teen-dee-HAHN	Hindî ko pô na iintindihan
Please repeat	ee-pa-kee-OO-leet NEEN-yo	Ipakiulit ninyo
Please speak slowly	mahg-sa-lee-TA po' ka-YO nahng ma-RA-hahn	Magsalita pô kayo ng marahan

LOCATION

When you need directions to get somewhere, you use the phrase meaning "Where is _____" and then add the words you need.

Where is _____?	na-sa-AHN _____?	Nasaan _____?
a restaurant	ahng rest-ow-RAHN	ang restaurant

13

English	Pronunciation	Tagalog Spelling
Where is a restaurant?	na-sa-AHN ahng rest-ow-RAHN?	Nasaan ang restaurant?
a hotel	ahng o-TEL	ang otel
Where is a hotel?	na-sa-AHN ahng o-TEL?	Nasaan ang otel?
railroad station	ahng est-ahss-YOAN nahng TREN	ang estasion ng tren
Where is the railroad station?	na-sa-AHN ahng est-ahss-YOAN nahng TREN?	Nasaan ang estasion ng tren?
a toilet?	ahng ka-SEEL-yahss	ang kasilyas
Where is a toilet?	na-sa-AHN ahng ka-SEEL-yahss?	Nasaan ang kasilyas?

DIRECTIONS

The answer to your question "Where is such and such?" may be "To the right" or "To the left" or "Straight ahead," so you need to know these phrases.

English	Pronunciation	Tagalog Spelling
To the right	sa ka-NAHN	Sa kanan
To the left	sa ka-lee-WA'	Sa kaliwâ
Straight ahead	sa oo-na-HAHN	Sa unahan

14

It is sometimes useful to say "Please point" or "Take me there."

Please point	ee-pa-kee-TOO-ro'	Ipakiturò
Take me there	sa-MA-hahn mo ah-KO do-OAN	Samahan mo ako doon

If you are driving and ask the distance to another town, it will be given to you in kilometers, not miles.

Kilometers	kee-LO-may-tro	Kilometro

One kilometer equals ⅝ of a mile.

NUMBERS

You need to know the numbers:

One	ee-SA	isa
Two	da-la-WA	dalawa
Three	taht-LO	tatlo
Four	AH-paht	apat
Five	lee-MA	lima
Six	AH-neem	anim
Seven	pee-TO	pito
Eight	wa-LO	walo
Nine	S⌣YAHM	siam

English	Pronunciation	Tagalog Spelling
Ten	sahm-POO'	sampû

For "eleven," "twelve," "thirteen," etc., you use the word "la-BEENG" followed by the word for "one," "two," "three," etc.

English	Pronunciation	Tagalog Spelling
Eleven	la-BEENG ee-SA	labing isa
Twelve	la-BEENG da-la-WA	labing dalawa
Thirteen	la-BEENG taht-LO	labing tatlo
Twenty	da-la-WAHNG POO'	dalawang pû

For "twenty-one," "twenty-two," etc., you say "twenty and one," "twenty and two," etc.

English	Pronunciation	Tagalog Spelling
Twenty-one	da-la-WAHNG POO' aht ee-SA	dalawang pû at isa
Twenty-two	da-la-WAHNG POO' aht da-la-WA	dalawang pû at dalawa
Thirty	taht-loong POO'	tatlung pû
Forty	AH-paht na POO'	apat na pû
Fifty	lee-mahng POO'	limang pû

18

English	Pronunciation	Tagalog Spelling
Sixty	AH-neem na POO'	anim na pû
Seventy	pee-toong POO'	pitung pû
Eighty	wa-loong POO'	walung pû
Ninety	s‿yahm na POO'	siam na pû
One hundred	ee-sahng da-AHN	isang daan
One thousand	ee-sahng LEE-bo	isang libo

19

WHAT'S THIS?

When you want to know the name of something, you can say "What's this?" and point to the thing you mean.

what	ah-NO	ano
this	ee-TO	ito
What's this?	ah-NO ee-TO?	Ano ito?

ASKING FOR THINGS

When you want something, use the phrase "I want _____" and then add the name of the thing wanted.

I want _____	GOO-sto KO nahng _____	Gusto ko ng _____
food	pahg-KA-een	pagkain
I want some food	GOO-sto KO nahng pahg-KA-een	Gusto ko ng pagkain
cigarettes	see-ga-reel-YO	sigarilyo
I want some cigarettes	GOO-sto KO nahng see-ga-reel-YO	Gusto ko ng sigarilyo
matches	PO-spo-ro	posporo
I want some matches	GOO-sto KO nahng PO-spo-ro	Gusto ko ng posporo

Here are the words for some of the things you may require:

water	TOO-beeg	tubig
bread	tee-NA-pa‿ee	tinapay
butter	mahn-tay-KEEL-ya	mantekilya
soup	SO-pahss	sopas
fish	eess-DA'	isdâ
meat *or* beef	kar-NAY	karne
pork	KAR-neeng BA-boy	karning baboy
lamb	KAR-neeng TOO-pa	karning tupa
chicken	ma-NOAK	manok
eggs	eet-LOAG	itlog
vegetables	GOO-la‿ee	gulay
potatoes	pa-TA-tahss	patatas
string beans	SEE-tow	sitaw
cabbage	ray-POAL-yo	repolyo
salad	en-sa-LA-da	ensalada
salt	ah-SEEN	asin
sugar	ah-SOO-kahl	asukal
fruit	PROO-tahss	prutas
bananas	SA-geeng	saging

English	Pronunciation	Tagalog Spelling
mangoes	mahng-GA	mangga
grapefruit	SOO-ha'	suhà
coconuts	BOO-ko	buko
chocolate	cho-ko-LA-tay	tsocolate
ice cream	sor-BET-ess	sorbetes
a cup of coffee	ee-sahng TA-sahng ka-PAY	isang tasang kape

MONEY

To find out how much things cost you say:

how much	mahg-KA-no	magkano
the cost	ahng ha-la-GA	ang halaga
How much does it cost?	mahg-KA-no ahng ha-la-GA?	Magkano ang halaga?

TIME

To find out what time it is, you say really, "What hour now?"

What time is it?	AH-noang O-rahss na?	Anong oras na?

22

English	Pronunciation	Tagalog Spelling

Tagalog speakers generally use Spanish phrases rather than Tagalog ones to tell time. [See pages 27 and 29.]

If you want to know when a movie starts, or when a train or bus leaves, you say:

what hour	AH-noang O-rahss	anong oras
the beginning	ahng see-moo-LA'	ang simulâ
of the movie	nahng SEE-nay	ng sine

English	*Pronunciation*	*Tagalog Spelling*
When does the movie start?	AH-noang O-rahss ahng see-moo-LA' nahng SEE-nay?	Anong oras ang simulâ ng sine?
the leaving	ahng ah-LEESS	ang alis
of the train	nahng TREN	ng tren
When does the train leave?	AH-noang O-rahss ahng ah-LEESS nahng TREN?	Anong oras ang alis ng tren?
of the bus	nahng owt-o-BOOSS	ng autobus
When does the bus leave?	AH-noang O-rahss ahng ah-LEESS nahng owt-o-BOOSS?	Anong oras ang alis ng autobus?
Yesterday	ka-HA-poan	kahapon
Today	nga-YOAN	ngayon

Notice the sound written "ng" in the last word. Listen again and repeat: "nga-YOAN, nga-YOAN." It is the same *ng*-sound that we have at the end of words like *sing, bring, ring,* but in Tagalog it also comes at the beginning of a word or syllable. Try just the sound again: "ng, ng; nga, nga."

English	Pronunciation	Tagalog Spelling
Tomorrow	BOO-kahss	bukas

The days of the week are:

Sunday	leeng-GO	linggo
Monday	LOO-ness	lunes
Tuesday	mar-TESS	martes
Wednesday	M‿YAYR-ko-less	mierkoles
Thursday	HWEB-ess	huebes
Friday	B‿YAYR-ness	biernes
Saturday	SA-ba-do	sabado

OTHER USEFUL PHRASES

The following phrases will be useful:

What is your name?	ah-NO ahng pa-NGA-lahn NEEN-yo?	Ano ang pangalan ninyo?
How do you say "table" (or anything else) in Tagalog?	ah-NO sa WEE-kahng ta-GA-loag ahng "table"?	Ano sa wikang tagalog ang "table"?
I am an American	ah-KO A‿ee ah-may-ree-KA-no	Ako ay Amerikano
I am your friend	ah-KO A‿ee ee-YOANG ka-ee-BEE-gahn	Ako ay iyong kaibigan

25

English	Pronunciation	Tagalog Spelling
Where is the nearest town?	na-sa-AHN ahng pee-na-ka-ma-LA-peet na BAR-yo DEET-o?	Nasaan ang pinakamalapit na barrio dito?
Which is the road to Manila?	sa-AHN ahng da-AHNG pa-TOONG-o sa ma⌣ee-NEE-la'?	Saan ang daang patungo sa Maynilà?
Please help me	pa-kee-too-LOONG-ahn NEEN-yo ah-KO	Pakitulungan ninyo ako
Good-by	pa-AH-lahm	Paalam

Tagalog speakers frequently use another expression which means "Long life." It is. "ma-BOO-ha⌣ee" (Mabuhay).

26

English	*Pronunciation*	*Tagalog Spelling*

The following Spanish phrases are used in telling time:

One o'clock	ah la OO-na	a la una
Two o'clock	ah lahss DOASS	a las dos
Three o'clock	ah lahss TRESS	a las tres
Four o'clock	ah lahss KWA-tro	a las cuatro
Five o'clock	ah lahss SEEN-ko	a las cinco
Six o'clock	ah lahss SAYSS	a las seis
Seven o'clock	ah lahss S‿YET-ay	a las siete
Eight o'clock	ah lahss O-cho	a las ocho
Nine o'clock	ah lahss NWEB-ay	a las nuebe
Ten o'clock	ah lahss D‿YESS	a las diez
Eleven o'clock	ah lahss OAN-say	a las once

WHAT'S THE TIME IN TAGALOG?

English	Pronunciation	Tagalog Spelling
Twelve o'clock	ah lahss DOASS-ay	a las doce
Ten past two	ah lahss DOASS ee D‿YESS	a las dos y diez
Quarter past three	ah lahss TRESS ee KWART-o	a las tres y cuarto
Half past four	ah lahss KWA-tro ee MED-ya	a las cuatro y media
Quarter of five	MEN-oass KWART-o pa-ra ah lahss SEEN-ko	menos cuarto para a las cinco
Ten of six	MEN-oass D‿YESS pa-ra ah lahss SAYSS	menos diez para a las seis

ADDITIONAL EXPRESSIONS

Come in!	too-LOY PO' ka-YO!	Tuloy pô kayo!
Have a seat	mow-PO' ka-YO	Maupô kayo
Glad to know you	ma-GOO-toass PO' ka-YO	Magutos pô kayo
I don't know	heen-DEE' ko po' ah-LAHM	Hindî ko pô alam
I think so	sa ah-KA-la ko po'	Sa akala ko pô
I don't think so	sa ah-KA-la koy po' heen-DEE'	Sa akala ko'y pô hindî
Maybe	ma-RA-heel	Marahil
Stop! *or* **Halt!**	TEEG-eel!	Tigil!
Come here!	ha-LEE-ka REE-to!	Halika rito!
Right away! *or* **Quickly!**	ah-GAHD!	Agad!
Come quickly!	poo-ma-REET-o ka-YO ah-GAHD!	Pumarito kayo agad!
Go quickly!	poo-ma-ro-OAN ka-YO ah-GAHD!	Pumaroon kayo agad!

I am hungry	ah-KO A⌣ee na-goo-GOO-toam	Ako ay nagugutom
I am thirsty	ah-KO A⌣ee na-oo-OO-how	Ako ay nauuhaw
I am tired	ah-KO A⌣ee pa-GOAD	Ako ay pagod
I am lost	ah-KO A⌣ee na-lee-GOW	Ako ay naligaw
Help!	TOO-loang!	Tulong!
Bring help!	koo-MOO-ha nahng TOO-loang!	Kumuha ng tulong!

English	Pronunciation	Tagalog Spelling
I will pay you	ba-ba-YA-rahn ko ka-YO	Babayaran ko kayo
Which way is north?	ah-LEEN ahng ee-LA-ya?	Alin ang ilaya?
south	TEE-moag	timog
east	see-LAHNG-ahn	silangan
west	kahn-LOO-rahn	kanluran
Draw me a map	ee-GOO-heet mo ah-KO nahng MA-pa	Iguhit mo ako ng mapa
Take me to the doctor	dahl-HEEN mo ah-KO sa doak-TOR	Dalhin mo ako sa doctor
Take me to the hospital	dahl-HEEN mo ah-KO sa o-spee-TAHL	Dalhin mo ako sa ospital

English	Pronunciation	Tagalog Spelling
Where is the town?	na-sa-AHN ahng BA-yahn?	Nasaan ang bayan?
Where is the camp?	na-sa-AHN ahng KAHM-po?	Nasaan ng kampo?
How far is it?	ga-AH-noang ka-LA-yo'?	Gaanong kalayô?
Is it far?	ma-LA-yo ba?	Malayo ba?
Is it near?	ma-LA-peet ba?	Malapit ba?
Danger!	pa-NGA-neeb!	Panganib!
Take cover!	MAHG-koo-blee ka-YO!	Magkubli kayo!
Gas!	GAHSS!	Gas!
Watch out!	mahg-EENG-aht ka-YO!	Magingat kayo!
Wait a minute!	heen-TA‿ee MOO-na!	Hintay muna!
It's here	nahn DEET-o	Nan dito
It's there	nahn dee-YAHN	Nan diyan
or	nahn do-OAN	Nan doon

FILL-IN SENTENCES

In this section you will find a number of sentences, each containing a blank space which can be filled in with any one of the words in the list that follows. For example, if you want to say "Where is a doctor?" find the fill-in sentence for "Where is a ____?" and, in the list following the sentences, the word for "doctor." Then combine them as follows:

Where is a ____?   na-sa-AHN   Nasaan ang ____?
                    ahng ____?

English	Pronunciation	Tagalog Spelling
doctor	doak-TOR	doctor
Where is a doctor?	na-sa-AHN ahng doak-TOR?	Nasaan ang doctor?
I want ___	GOO-sto KO nahng ___	Gusto ko ng ___
We want ___	GOO-sto NA-meen nahng ___	Gusto namin ng ___
Give me ___	beeg-YAHN neen-yo ah-KO nahng ___	Bigyan ninyo ako ng ___
Bring me ___	dahl-HAHN neen-yo ah-KO nahng ___	Dalhan ninyo ako ng ___
Where can I get ___?	sa-AHN ah-KO ma-ka-ka-KOO-ha nahng ___?	Saan ako makakakuha ng ___?
I have ___	ah-KO A‿ee ma‿ee-ro-OANG ___	Ako ay mayroong ___
We have ___	ka-MEE A‿ee ma‿ee-ro-OANG ___	Kami ay mayroong ___
I don't have ___	ah-KO A‿ee wa-LAHNG ___	Ako ay walang ___

35

English	Pronunciation	Tagalog Spelling
We don't have ____	ka-MEE A‿ee wa-LAHNG ____	Kami ay walang ____
Have you ____?	ma‿ee-ro-OAN ba ka-YOANG ____?	ɔon ba kayong __ __ʔ

Example:

English	Pronunciation	Tagalog Spelling
I want ____	GOO-sto KO nahng ____	Gusto ko ng ____
drinking water	ee-noo-MEEN	inumin
I want drinking water	GOO-sto KO nahng ee-noo-MEEN	Gusto ko ng inumin
beer	sayr-BESS-ah	serbesa
boiled water	pee-na-koo-LOANG TOO-beeg	pinakulong tubig
breadfruit	NAHNG-ka'	nangkâ
cheese	KESS-o	keso
ham	ha-MOAN	hamon
lemons	lee-MOAN	limon
milk	GA-tahss	gatas
onions	see-BOO-yahss	sibuyas

English	Pronunciation	Tagalog Spelling
oranges	da-lahng-HEE-ta	dalanghita
papayas	pa-PA-ya	papaya
pineapple	peen-YA	piña
tea	CHA	tsa
a cup	TA-sa	tasa
a fork	ten-ay-DOR	tenedor
a glass	BA-so	baso
a knife	koo-CHEEL-yo	kutsilyo
a plate	PLA-to	plato
a spoon	koo-CHA-ra	kutsara
a bed	KA-tray	katre
a mattress	koo-CHOAN	kutson

English	Pronunciation	Tagalog Spelling
a mosquito net	koo-lahm-BO'	kulambô
a pillow	OO-nahn	unan
a room	KWART-o	kwarto
sheets *or* blankets	KOO-moat	kumot
a towel	TWAHL-ya	twalya
cigars	ta-BA-ko	tabako
a pipe	PEE-pa	pipa
pipe tobacco	DA-hoan nahng ta-BA-ko	dahon ng tabako
ink	TEEN-ta	tinta
paper	pa-PEL	papel
a pen	PLOO-ma	pluma
a pencil	LA-peess	lapis
a comb	sook-LA⌣ee	suklay
hot water	ma-EEN-eet na TOO-beeg	mainit na tubig
a razor	la-BA-sa	labasa
razor blades	ta-LEEM nahng la-BA-sa	talim ng labasa

WHICH IS WHICH?

TOOTHBRUSH

SOAP

sa-BOAN
la-BA-sa
TWAHL-ya
say-PEEL-yo nahng NGEEP-een

RAZOR

TOWEL

(Answers on pages 38-40)

English	Pronunciation	Tagalog Spelling
a shaving brush	BRO-cha	brotsa
shaving soap	sa-BOANG pahng-AH-heet	sabong pangahit
soap	sa-BOAN	sabon
a toothbrush	say-PEEL-yo nahng NGEEP-een	sepilyo ng ngipin
toothpaste	PA-stahng pahng-LEE-neess nahng NGEEP-een	pastang panglinis ng ngipin
a hand-kerchief	pahn-YO	panyo
a raincoat	ka-PO-tay	kapote
a shirt	ka-mee-sa-DEN-tro	kamisadentro
shoelaces	TA-lee nahng sa-PA-toass	tali ng sapatos
shoe polish	pahng-pa-keen-TAHB nahng sa-PA-toass	pangpakintab ng sapatos
shoes	sa-PA-toass	sapatos
an undershirt	ka-mee-SET-ah	kamiseta
undershorts	sa-la-WAHL	salawal

English	Pronunciation	Tagalog Spelling
buttons	boo-TOAN-ess	butones
a needle	ka-RA-yoam	karayom
pins	AH-spee-lee	aspili
safety pins	payr-DEE-blay	perdible
thread	see-NOO-leed	sinulid
adhesive tape	BEN-dahng pahng-dee-KEET	bendang pangdikit
an antiseptic	ahn-tee-SEP-tee-ko	antiseptico
aspirin	ah-spee-REE-na	aspirina
a bandage	ben-DA-hay	bendahe
cotton	BOO-lahk	bulak
a disinfectant	dee-seen-fek-TAHN-tay	disinfectante
iodine	teen-TOO-ra day YO-do	tintura de iodo
a laxative	poor-GA	purga
gasoline	ga-so-LEE-na	gasolina

I want to ___	GOO-sto koang ___	Gusto kong ___
We want to ___	GOO-sto NA-meeng ___	Gusto naming ___

English	Pronunciation	Tagalog Spelling
Do you want to ____?	GOO-sto ba neen-YOANG ____?	Gusto ba ninyong ____?
Example:		
I want to ____	GOO-sto koang ____	Gusto kong ____
eat	koo-MA-een	kumain
I want to eat	GOO-sto koang koo-MA-een	Gusto kong kumain
be shaved	mahg-pa-AH-heet	magpaahit
buy this	beel-HEEN ee-TO	bilhin ito
drink	oo-mee-NOAM	uminom
have a haircut	mahg-pa-goo-PEET	magpagupit
pay	mahg-BA-yahd	magbayad
rest	mahg-pa-hee-NGA	magpahinga
sleep	ma-TOO-loag	matulog
take a bath	ma-LEE-go	maligo
wash up	mahg-HOO-gahss	maghugas
Where is the ____? *or* Where is a ____?	na-sa-AHN ahng ____?	Nasaan ang ____?

English	Pronunciation	Tagalog Spelling
How far is the ____? *or* How far is a ____?	ga-AH-noang ka-LA-yo' ahng ____?	Gaanong kalayô ang ____?
Example:		
Where is a ____?	na-sa-AHN ahng ____?	Nasaan ang ____?
barber	bar-BAY-ro	barbero
Where is a barber?	na-sa-AHN ahng bar-BAY-ro?	Nasaan ang barbero?
dentist	den-TEE-sta	dentista
doctor	doak-TOR	doctor
mechanic	may-KA-nee-ko	mekaniko
policeman	poo-LEESS	pulis
porter	por-TAY-ro	portero
servant	ah-LEE-la'	alilà
shoemaker	sa-pa-TAY-ro	sapatero
tailor	SA-stray	sastre
workman	mahng-ga-GA-wa'	manggagawâ
bridge	too-LA‿ee	tulay
bus	owt-o-BOOSS	autobus
camp	KAHM-po	kampo

43

English	Pronunciation	Tagalog Spelling
church	seem-BA-hahn	simbahan
city	see-oo-DAHD	siudad
clothing store	ahl-ma-SEN	almasen
drugstore *or* pharmacy	bo-TEE-ka	botika
garage	ga-RA-hay	garahe
gas station	est-ahss-YOAN nahng ga-so-LEE-na	estasion ng gasolina
grocery	"grocery"	grosery
highway	da-AHN	daan
hospital	o-spee-TAHL	ospital
house	BA-ha‿ee	bahay
laundry	la-bahn-day-REE-ah	labanderia
main street	KAHL-yay ray-AHL	kalye real
market place	pa-LENG-kay	palengke
police station	est-ahss-YOAN nahng po-LEESS-ya	estasion ng polisia
post office	"post office"	post office
railroad	da-AHN nahng TREN	daan ng tren

WHICH IS WHICH?

BRIDGE

BANDAGE

ben-DA-hay
too-LA⌣ee
tay-LEP-o-no
da-AHN nahng TREN

RAILROAD

TELEPHONE

(Answers on pages 41-46)

English	Pronunciation	Tagalog Spelling
river	EE-loag	ilog
road	da-AHN	daan
settlement	BAR-yo	barrio
spring	boo-KAHL	bukal
streetcar	trahm-BEE-ya	trambiya
telephone	tay-LEP-o-no	telepono
town	BA-yahn	bayan
well	ba-LOAN	balon

I am ___	ah-KO A‿ee ___	Ako ay ___
He is ___	see-YA A‿ee ___	Siya ay ___
We are ___	ka-MEE A‿ee ___	Kami ay ___
They are ___	see-LA A‿ee ___	Sila ay ___
Are you ___?	ee-KOW ba A‿ee ___?	Ikaw ba ay ___?

English	Pronunciation	Tagalog Spelling
Example:		
I am ____	ah-KO A⌣ee ____	Ako ay ____
sick	ma⌣ee-sa-KEET	maysakit
I am sick	ah-KO A⌣ee ma⌣ee-sa-KEET	Ako ay maysakit
hungry	na-goo-GOO-toam	nagugutom
lost	na-lee-GOW	naligaw
thirsty	na-oo-OO-how	nauuhaw
tired	pa-GOAD	pagod
wounded	na-soo-GA-tahn	nasugatan

English	Pronunciation	Tagalog Spelling
It is ——	ee-YAHN A⌣ee ——	Iyan ay ——
Is it ——?	ee-YAHN ba A⌣ee ——?	Iyan ba ay ——?
It is not ——	ee-YAHN A⌣ee heen-DEE' ——	Iyan ay hindî ——
It is too —— or It is very ——	ee-YAHN A⌣ee mahss-YA-doang ——	Iyan ay masiadong ———
This is ——	ee-TO A⌣ee ——	Ito ay ——
That is ——	ee-YOAN A⌣ee ——	Iyon ay ——

Example:

It is ——	ee-YAHN A⌣ee ——	Iyan ay ——
good	ma-BOO-tay	mabute
It is good	ee-YAHN A⌣ee ma-BOO-tay	Iyan ay mabute
bad	ma-sa-MA'	masamâ
cheap	MOO-ra	mura
expensive	ma-HAHL	mahal

48

English	Pronunciation	Tagalog Spelling
large	ma-la-KAY	malake
small	ma-lee-EET	maliit
clean	ma-LEE-neess	malinis
dirty	ma-roo-MEE	marumi
cold	ma-la-MEEG	malamig
hot	ma-EE-neet	mainit
much	ma-RA-mee	marami
enough	HOO-sto na	husto na
	or sa-paht NA	sapat na

ALPHABETICAL
WORD LIST

English	*Pronunciation*	*Tagalog Spelling*
	A	
adhesive tape	BEN-dahng pahng-dee-KEET	bendang pangdikit
afternoon	HA-poan	hapon
Good after-noon	ma-gahn-DAHNG HA-poan PO'	Magandang hapon pô
American		
I am an American	ah-KO A-ee ah-may-ree-KA-no	Ako ay Amerikano
and	aht	at
antiseptic	ahn-tee-SEP-tee-ko	antiseptico
Are you ___?	ee-KOW ba A⌣ee ___?	Ikaw ba ay ___
aspirin	ah-spee-REE-na	aspirina
	B	
bad	ma-sa-MA'	masamâ
bananas	SA-geeng	saging
bandage	ben-DA-hay	bendahe

barber	bar-BAY-ro	barbero
bath		
I want to take a bath	GOO-sto koang ma-LEE-go	Gusto kong mali-go
bed	KA-tray	katre
beef	kar-NAY	karne
beer	sayr-BESS-ah	serbesa
blades		
razor blades	ta-LEEM nahng la-BA-sa	talim ng labasa
blankets	KOO-moat	kumot
bread	tee-NA-pa‿ee	tinapay

51

English	Pronunciation	Tagalog Spelling
breadfruit	NAHNG-ka'	nangkâ
bridge	too-LA‿ee	tulay
bring		
Bring help!	koo-MOO-ha nahng TOO-loang!	Kumuha ng tulong!
Bring me ___	dahl-HAHN neen-yo ah-KO nahng ___	Dalhan ninyo ako ng ___
brush		
shaving brush	BRO-cha	brotsa
bus	owt-o-BOOSS	autobus
When does the bus leave?	AH-noang O-rahss ahng ah-LEESS nahng owt-o-BOOSS?	Anong oras ang alis ng autobus?
butter	mahn-tay-KEEL-ya	mantekilya
buttons	boo-TOAN-ess	butones
buy		
I want to buy this	GOO-sto koang beel-HEEN ee-TO	Gusto kong bilhin ito

English	Pronunciation	Tagalog Spelling
	C	
cabbage	ray-POAL-yo	repolyo
camp	KAHM-po	kampo
Where is the camp?	na-sa-AHN ahng KAHM-po?	Nasaan ang kampo?
cheap	MOO-ra	mura
cheese	KESS-o	keso
chicken	ma-NOAK	manok
chocolate	cho-ko-LA-tay	tsocolate
church	seem-BA-hahn	simbahan
cigarettes	see-ga-reel-YO	sigarilyo

WHICH IS WHICH?

CHEESE

BREAD

tee-NA-pa‿ee
KESS-o
ka-PAY
KA-tray

BED

COFFEE

(Answers in Word List)

English	Pronunciation	Tagalog Spelling
I want some cigarettes	GOO-sto KO nahng see-ga-reel-YO	Gusto ko ng sigarilyo
cigars	ta-BA-ko	tabako
city	see-oo-DAHD	siudad
clean	ma-LEE-neess	malinis
clothing store	ahl-ma-SEN	almasen
coconuts	BOO-ko or nee-YOAG	buko niyog
coffee	ka-PAY	kape
cold	ma-la-MEEG	malamig
comb	sook-LA‿ee	suklay
come		
Come here!	ha-LEE-ka REE-to!	Halika rito!
Come in!	too-LOY PO' ka-YO!	Tuloy pô kayo!
Come quickly!	poo-ma-REET-o ka-YO ah-GAHD!	Pumarito kayo agad!
cost		
How much does it cost?	mahg-KA-no ahng ha-la-GA?	Magkano ang halaga?
cotton	BOO-lahk	bulak

55

English	Pronunciation	Tagalog Spelling
cover		
Take cover!	MAHG-koo-blee ka-YO!	Magkubli kayo!
cup	TA-sa	tasa
a cup of coffee	ee-sahng TA-sahng ka-PAY	isang tasang kape

D

English	Pronunciation	Tagalog Spelling
Danger!	pa-NGA-neeb!	Panganib!
dentist	den-TEE-sta	dentista
dirty	ma-roo-MEE	marumi
disinfectant	dee-seen-fek-TAHN-tay	disinfectante
doctor	doak-TOR	doctor
Take me to the doctor	dahl-HEEN mo ah-KO sa doak-TOR	Dalhin mo ako sa doctor
Draw me a map	ee-GOO-heet mo ah-KO nahng MA-pa	Iguhit mo ako ng mapa
drink		
I want to drink	GOO-sto koang oo-mee-NOAM	Gusto kong uminom
drugstore (pharmacy)	bo-TEE-ka	botika

56

English	Pronunciation	Tagalog Spelling
	E	
east	see-LAHNG-ahn	silangan
eat		
I want to eat	GOO-sto koang koo-MA-een	Gusto kong kumain
eggs	eet-LOAG	itlog
eight	wa-LO	walo
eighty	wa-loong POO'	walung pû
eleven	la-BEENG ee-SA	labing isa
enough	HOO-sto na	husto na
	or sa-paht NA	sapat na
evening	ga-BEE	gabí
Good evening	ma-gahn-DAHNG ga-BEE PO'	Magandang gabí pô
Excuse me	pa-TA-wahd po'	Patawad pô
expensive	ma-HAHL	mahal
	F	
far		
How far is it?	ga-AH-noang ka-LA-yo'?	Gaanong kalayô?
How far is the (a) ____?	ga-AH-noang ka-LA-yo' ahng ____?	Gaanong kalayô ang ____?

English	Pronunciation	Tagalog Spelling
Is it far?	ma-LA-yo ba?	Malayo ba?
fifty	lee-mahng POO'	limang pû
fine	ma-BOO-tay	mabute
fish	eess-DA'	isdâ
five	lee-MA	lima
food	pahg-KA-een	pagkain
I want some food	GOO-sto KO nahng pahg-KA-een	Gusto ko ng pagkain
fork	ten-ay-DOR	tenedor
forty	AH-paht na POO'	apat na pû
four	AH-paht	apat
Friday	B‿YAYR-ness	biernes
friend		
I am your friend	ah-KO A‿ee ee-YOANG ka-ee-BEE-gahn	Ako ay iyong kaibigan
fruit	PROO-tahss	prutas

G

garage	ga-RA-hay	garahe
gas!	GAHSS!	Gas!

English	Pronunciation	Tagalog Spelling
gasoline	ga-so-LEE-na	gasolina
gas station	est-ahss-YOAN nahng ga-so-LEE-na	estasion ng gasolina
get		
Where can I get ____?	sa-AHN ah-KO ma-ka-ka-KOO-ha nahng ____?	Saan ako makakakuha ng ____?
Give me ____	beeg-YAHN neen-yo ah-KO nahng ____	Bigyan ninyo ako ng ____
Glad to know you	ma-GOO-toass PO' ka-YO	Magutos pô kayo
glass	BA-so	baso
good	ma-BOO-tay	mabute
Good afternoon	ma-gahn-DAHNG HA-poan PO'	Magandang hapon ‚pô
Good-by	pa-AH-lahm	Paalam
Good evening	ma-gahn-DAHNG ga-BEE PO'	Magandang gabí pô
Good morning	ma-gahn-DAHNG oo-MA-ga PO'	Magandang umaga pô
grapefruit	SOO-ha'	suhà

59

English	Pronunciation	Tagalog Spelling

H

haircut

  I want to have a haircut — GOO-sto koang mahg-pa-goo-PEET — Gusto kong magpa-gupit

Halt! — TEEG-eel! — Tigil!

ham — ha-MOAN — hamon

handkerchief — pahn-YO — panyo

Have a seat — mow-PO' ka-YO — Maupô kayo

Have you ____? — ma‿ee-ro-OAN ba ka-YOANG ____? — Mayroon ba kayong ____?

he — see-YA — siya

  He is ____ — see-YA A‿ee ____ — Siya ay ____

Help! — TOO-loang! — Tulong!

  Bring help! — koo-MOO-ha nahng TOO-loang! — Kumuha ng tulong!

  Please help me — pa-kee-too-LOONG-ahn NEEN-yo ah-KO — Pakitulungan ninyo ako

English	Pronunciation	Tagalog Spelling
here	DEET-o	dito
It's here	nahn DEET-o	Nan dito
highway	da-AHN	daan
hospital	o-spee-TAHL	ospital
Take me to the hospital	dahl-HEEN mo ah-KO sa o-spee-tahl	Dalhin mo ako sa ospital
hot	ma-EE-neet	mainit
hotel	o-TEL	otel
Where is a hotel?	na-sa-AHN ahng o-TEL?	Nasaan ang otel?
hour	O-rahss	oras
house	BA-ha⌣ee	bahay
how		
How are you?	ka-moo-sta PO' ka-YO?	Kamusta pô kayo?
How do you say "table" in Tagalog?	ah-NO sa WEE-kahng ta-GA-loag ahng "table"?	Ano sa wikang ta-galog ang "table"?
How far is the ____? or How far is a ____?	ga-AH-noang ka-LA-yo' ahng ____?	Gaano kalayô ang ____?

61

English	Pronunciation	Tagalog Spelling
How much?	mahg-KA-no?	magkano?
How much does it cost?	mahg-KA-no ahng ha-la-GA?	Magkano ang halaga?
hundred		
one hundred	ee-sahng da-AHN	isang daan
hungry	na-goo-GOO-toam	nagugutom
I am hungry	ah-KO A̮ee na-goo-GOO-toam	Ako ay nagugutom

I

English	Pronunciation	Tagalog Spelling
I	ah-KO	ako
I am___	ah-KO A̮ee ___	Ako ay ___
I have ___	ah-KO A̮ee ma̮ee-ro-OANG ___	Ako ay may-roong ___
I don't have ___	ah-KO A̮ee wa-LAHNG ___	Ako ay walang ___
I want ___	GOO-sto KO nahng ___	Gusto ko ng ___
I want to ___	GOO-sto koang ___	Gusto kong ___
ice cream	sor-BET-ess	sorbetes
ink	TEEN-ta	tinta
iodine	teen-TOO-ra day YO-do	tintura de iodo

English	Pronunciation	Tagalog Spelling
is		
It is ____	ee-YAHN A⌣ee ____	Iyan ay ____
Is it ____?	ee-YAHN ba A⌣ee ____?	Iyan ba ay ____?
It is not ____	ee-YAHN A⌣ee heen-DEE' ____	Iyan ay hindî ____
It is too ____ or It is very ____	ee-YAHN A⌣ee mahss-YA-doang ____	Iyan ay masia-dong ____
it	ee-YAHN	iyan

K

English	Pronunciation	Tagalog Spelling
kilometers	kee-LO-may-tro	kilometro
knife	koo-CHEEL-yo	kutsilyo
know		
Glad to know you	ma-GOO-toass PO' ka-YO	Magutos pô kayo
I don't know	heen-DEE' ko po' ah-LAHM	Hindî ko pô alam

L

English	Pronunciation	Tagalog Spelling
lamb	KAR-neeng TOO-pa	karning tupa
large	ma-la-KAY	malake

WHICH IS WHICH?

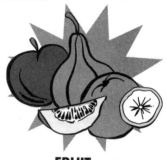

FRUIT

HOUSE

BA-ha‿ee
koo-CHEEL-yo
eet-LOAG
PROO-tahss

KNIFE

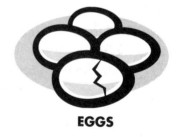

EGGS

(Answers in Word List)

English	Pronunciation	Tagalog Spelling
laundry	la-bahn-day-REE-ah	labanderia
laxative	poor-GA	purga
leave		
When does the bus leave?	AH-noang O-rahss ahng ah-LEESS nahng owt-o-BOOSS?	Anong oras ang alis ng autobus?
When does the train leave?	AH-noang O-rahss ahng ah-LEESS nahng TREN?	Anong oras ang alis ng tren?
left		
To the left	sa ka-lee-WA	Sa kaliwâ
lemons	lee-MOAN	limon
Long life	ma-BOO-ha‿ee	Mabuhay
lost	na-lee-GOW	naligaw
I am lost	ah-KO A‿ee na-lee-GOW	Ako ay naligaw

M

main street	KAHL-yay ray-AHL	kalye real
mangoes	mahng-GA	mangga
map	MA-pa	mapa

65

English	Pronunciation	Tagalog Spelling
Draw me a map	ee-GOO-heet mo ah-KO nahng MA-pa	Iguhit mo ako ng mapa
market place	pa-LENG-kay	palengke
matches	PO-spo-ro	posporo
I want some matches	GOO-sto KO nahng PO-spo-ro	Gusto ko ng pospo-ro
mattress	koo-CHOAN	kutson
maybe	ma-RA-heel	marahil
meat	kar-NAY	karne
mechanic	may-KA-nee-ko	mekaniko
milk	GA-tahss	gatas
minute		
Wait a minute!	heen-TA⌣ee MOO-na!	Hintay muna!
Miss	bee-nee-BEE-neeng	Binibining
Monday	LOO-ness	lunes
morning	oo-MA-ga	umaga
Good morning	ma-gahn-DAHNG oo-MA-ga PO'	magandang umaga pô
mosquito net	koo-lahm-BO'	kulambô
movie	SEE-nay	sine

English	Pronunciation	Tagalog Spelling
When does the movie start?	AH-noang O-rahss ahng see-moo-LA' nahng SEE-nay?	Anong oras ang simulâ ng sine?
Mr.	geen-o-OANG	Ginoong
Mrs.	GEEN-ahng	Ginang
much	ma-RA-mee	marami

N

name		
What is your name?	ah-NO ahng pa-NGA-lahn NEEN-yo?	Ano ang pangalan ninyo?
near		
Is it near?	ma-LA-peet ba?	Malapit ba?
the nearest town	ahng pee-na-ka-ma-LA-peet na BAR-yo	ang pinakamalapit na barrio
needle	ka-RA-yoam	karayom
nine	S⌣YAHM	siam
ninety	s⌣yahm na POO'	siam na pû
no	heen-DEE' po'	hindî pô
north	ee-LA-ya	ilaya

English	Pronunciation	Tagalog Spelling
Which way is north?	ah-LEEN ahng ee-LA-ya?	Alin ang ilaya?

O

English	Pronunciation	Tagalog Spelling
one	ee-SA	Isa
onions	see-BOO-yahss	sibuyas
oranges	da-lahng-HEE-ta	dalanghita

P

English	Pronunciation	Tagalog Spelling
papayas	pa-PA-ya	papaya
paper	pa-PEL	papel
pay		
I want to pay	GOO-sto koang mahg-BA-yahd	Gusto kong magbayad
I will pay you	ba-ba-YA-rahn ko ka-YO	Babayaran ko kayo
pen	PLOO-ma	pluma
pencil	LA-peess	lapis
pharmacy	bo-TEE-ka	botika
pillow	OO-nahn	unan
pineapple	peen-YA	piña
pins	AH-spee-lee	aspili
safety pins	payr-DEE-blay	perdible

WHICH IS WHICH?

PLATE

NEEDLE

PLA-to
LA-pees
ka-RA-yoam
ka-SEEL-yahss

PENCIL

TOILET

(Answers in Word List)

English	Pronunciation	Tagalog Spelling
pipe	PEE-pa	pipa
pipe tobacco	DA-hoan nahng ta-BA-ko	dahon ng tabako
plate	PLA-to	plato
please	pa-kee-SOO-yo'	pakisuyò
Please repeat	ee-pa-kee-OO-leet NEEN-yo	Ipakiulit ninyo
Please speak slowly	mahg-sa-lee-TA po' ka-YO nahng ma-RA-hahn	Magsalita pô kayo ng marahan
point		
Please point	ee-pa-kee-TOO-ro'	Ipakiturò
police station	est-ahss-YOAN nahng po-LEESS-ya	estasion ng polisia
policeman	poo-LEESS	pulis
polish		
shoe polish	pahng-pa-keen-TAHB nahng sa-PA-toass	pangpakintab ng sapatos
pork	KAR-neeng BA-boy	karning baboy
porter	por-TAY-ro	portero
potatoes	pa-TA-tahss	patatas

English	Pronunciation	Tagalog Spelling
	Q	
Quickly!	ah-GAHD!	Agad!
Come quickly!	poo-ma-REET-o ka-YO ah-GAHD!	Pumarito kayo agad!
Go quickly!	poo-ma-ro-OAN ka-YO ah-GAHD!	Pumaroon kayo agad!
	R	
railroad	da-AHN nahng TREN	daan ng tren
railroad station	est-ahss-YOAN nahng TREN	estasion ng tren
Where is the railroad station?	na-sa-AHN ahng est-ahss-YOAN nahng TREN?	Nasaan ang estasion ng tren?
raincoat	ka-PO-tay	kapote
razor	la-BA-sa	labasa
razor blades	ta-LEEM nahng la-BA-sa	talim ng labasa
repeat		
Please repeat	ee-pa-kee-OO-leet NEEN-yo	Ipakiulit ninyo

71

English	Pronunciation	Tagalog Spelling
rest		
I want to rest	GOO-sto koang mahg-pa-hee-NGA	Gusto kong magpahinga
restaurant	rest-ow-RAHN	restaurant
Where is a restaurant?	na-sa-AHN ahng rest-ow-RAHN	Nasaan ang restaurant?
right		
To the right	sa ka-NAHN	Sa kanan
Right away!	ah-GAHD!	Agad!
river	EE-loag	ilog
road	da-AHN	daan
Which is the road to Manila?	sa-AHN ahng da-AHNG pa-TOONG-o sa ma⌣ee-NEE-la'?	Saan ang daang patungo sa Maynilà?
room	KWART-o	kwarto

S

English	Pronunciation	Tagalog Spelling
safety pins	payr-DEE-blay	perdible
sailors	mah-REE-no	marino

English	Pronunciation	Tagalog Spelling
Where are the sailors?	na-sa-AHN ahng ma-NGA mah-REE-no?	Nasaan ang mga marino?
salad	en-sa-LA-da	ensalada
salt	ah-SEEN	asin
Saturday	SA-ba-do	sabado
seat		
Have a seat	mow-PO' ka-YO	Maupô kayo
servant	ah-LEE-la'	alilà
settlement	BAR-yo	barrio
seven	pee-TO	pito
seventy	pee-toong POO'	pitung pû
shave		
shaving brush	BRO-cha	brotsa
shaving soap	sa-BOANG pahng-AH-heet	sabong pangahit
I want to be shaved	GOO-sto koang mahg-pa-AH-heet	Gusto kong magpaahit
sheets	KOO-moat	kumot
shirt	ka-mee-sa-DEN-tro	kamisadentro

English	Pronunciation	Tagalog Spelling
shoelaces	TA-lee nahng sa-PA-toass	tali ng sapatos
shoemaker	sa-pa-TAY-ro	sapatero
shoe polish	pahng-pa-keen-TAHB nahng sa-PA-toass	pangpakintab ng sapatos
shoes	sa-PA-toass	sapatos
sick	ma⏝ee-sa-KEET	maysakit
six	AH-neem	anim
sixty	AH-neem na POO'	anim na pû
sleep	ma-TOO-loag	matulog
slowly		
Please speak slowly	mahg-sa-lee-TA po' ka-YO nahng ma-RA-hahn	Magsalita pô kayo ng marahan
small	ma-lee-EET	maliit
soap	sa-BOAN	sabon
shaving soap	sa-BOANG pahng-AH-heet	sabong pangahit
soup	SO-pahss	sopas

English	Pronunciation	Tagalog Spelling
south	TEE-moag	timog
speak		
Please speak slowly	mahg-sa-lee-TA po' ka-YO nahng ma-RA-hahn	Magsalita pô kayo ng marahan
spoon	koo-CHA-ra	kutsara
spring *(of water)*	boo-KAHL	bukal
start		
When does the movie start?	AH-noang O-rahss ahng see-moo-LA' nahng SEE-nay?	Anong oras ang simulâ ng sine?
station		
police station	est-ahss-YOAN nahng po-LEESS-ya	estasion ng polisia
railroad station	est-ahss-YOAN nahng TREN	estasion ng tren
Stop!	TEEG-eel!	Tigil!
store		
clothing store	ahl-ma-SEN	Almasen
drugstore	bo-TEE-ka	botika
Straight ahead	sa oo-na-HAHN	Sa unahan

English	Pronunciation	Tagalog Spelling
street		
main street	KAHL-yay ray-AHL	kalye real
streetcar	trahm-BEE-ya	trambiya
string beans	SEE-tow	sitaw
sugar	ah-SOO-kahl	asukal
Sunday	leeng-GO	linggo

T

English	Pronunciation	Tagalog Spelling
tailor	SA-stray	sastre
take		
Take cover!	MAHG-koo-blee ka-YO!	Magkubli kayo!
Take me there	sa-MA-hahn mo ah-KO do-OAN	Samahan mo ako doon
Take me to the doctor	dahl-HEEN mo ah-KO sa doak-TOR	Dalhin mo ako sa doctor
Take me to the hospital	dahl-HEEN mo ah-KO sa o-spee-TAHL	Dalhin mo ako sa ospital
tea	CHA	tsa
telephone	tay-LEP-o-no	telepono
ten	sahm-POO	sampû

English	Pronunciation	Tagalog Spelling
thank you	sa-LA-maht po'	Salamat pô
that	ee-YOAN	iyon
That is ___	ee-YOAN A⌣ee ___	Iyon ay ___
there	dee-YAHN *or* do-OAN	diyan doon
It's there	nahn dee-YAHN *or* nahn do-OAN	Nan diyan Nan doon
they	see-LA	sila
They are ___	see-LA A⌣ee ___	Sila ay ___
think		
I think so	sa ah-KA-la ko po'	Sa akala ko pô
I don't think so	sa ah-KA-la koy po' heen-DEE'	Sa akala ko'y pô hindî
thirsty	na-oo-OO-how	nauuhaw
I am thirsty	ah-KO A⌣ee na-oo-OO-how	Ako ay nauuhaw
thirteen	la-BEENG taht-LO	labing tatlo
thirty	taht-loong POO'	ratlung pû
this	ee-TO	ito

WHICH IS WHICH?

SHOES

SPOON

koo-CHA-ra
sa-PA-toass
ah-SEEN
CHA

SALT

TEA

(Answers in Word List)

English	Pronunciation	Tagalog Spelling
This is ___	ee-TO A‿ee ___	Ito ay ___
What's this?	ah-NO ee-TO?	Ano ito?
thousand		
one thousand	ee-sahng LEE-bo	isang libo
thread	see-NOO-leed	sinulid
three	taht-LO	tatlo
Thursday	HWEB-ess	huebes
time		
What time is it?	AH-noang O-rahss na?	Anong oras na?
tired	pa-GOAD	pagod
I am tired	ah-KO A‿ee pa-GOAD	Ako ay pagod
today	nga-YOAN	ngayon
toilet	ka-SEEL-yahss	kasilyas
Where is a toilet?	na-sa-AHN ahng ka̅-SEEL-yahss?	Nasaan ang kasilyas?
tomorrow	BOO-kahss	bukas
toothbrush	say-PEEL-yo nahng NGEEP-een	sepilyo ng ngipin
toothpaste	PA-stahng pahng-LEE-neess nahng NGEEP-een	pastang panglinis ng ngipin

English	Pronunciation	Tagalog Spelling
towel	TWAHL-ya	twalya
town	BA-yahn	bayan
Where is the nearest town?	na-sa-AHN ahng pee-na-ka-ma-LA-peet na BAR-yo DEET-o?	Nasaan ang pinakamalapit na barrio dito?
Where is the town?	na-sa-AHN ahng BA-yahn?	Nasaan ang bayan?
train	TREN	tren
When does the train leave?	AH-noang O-rahss ahng ah-LEESS nahng TREN?	Anong oras ang alis ng tren?
Tuesday	mar-TESS	martes
twelve	la-BEENG da-la-WA	labing dalawa
twenty	da-la-WAHNG POO'	dalawang pû
twenty-one	da-la-WAHNG POO' aht ee-SA	dalawang pû at isa
twenty-two	da-la-WAHNG POO' aht da-la-WA	dalawang pû at dalawa
two	da-la-WA	dalawa

English	Pronunciation	Tagalog Spelling
	U	
undershirt	ka-mee-SET-ah	kamiseta
undershorts	sa-la-WAHL	salawal
understand		
Do you understand?	na ee-een-teen-dee-HAHN ba NEEN-yo?	Na iintindihan ba ninyo?
I don't understand?	heen-DEE' ko po' na ee-een-teen-dee-HAHN	Hindî ko pô na iintindihan
	V	
vegetables	GOO-la‿ee	gulay
	W	
Wait a minute!	heen-TA‿ee MOO-na!	Hintay muna!
want		
Do you want to ___?	GOO-sto ba neen-YOANG ___?	Gusto ba ninyong ___?
I want ___	GOO-sto KO nahng ___	Gusto ko ng ___
I want to ___	GOO-sto koang ___	Gusto kong ___

English	Pronunciation	Tagalog Spelling
We want ____	GOO-sto NA-meen nahng ____	Guston namin ng ____
We want to ____	GOO-sto NA-meeng ____	Gusto naming ____
wash		
I want to wash up	GOO-sto koang mahg-HOO-gahss	Gusto kong maghugas
Watch out!	mahg-EENG-aht ka-YO!	Magingat kayo!
water	TOO-beeg	tubig
boiled water	pee-na-koo-LOANG TOO-beeg	pinakulong tubig
drinking water	ee-noo-MEEN	inumin
hot water	ma-EEN-eet na TOO-beeg	mainit na tubig
we	ka-MEE	kami
We are ____	ka-MEE A‿ee ____	Kami ay ____
We don't have ____	ka-MEE A‿ee wa-LAHNG ____	Kami ay walang ____
We have ____	ka-MEE A‿ee ma‿ee-ro-OANG ____	Kami ay may-roong ____

English	Pronunciation	Tagalog Spelling
We want ___	GOO-sto NA-meen nahng ___	Gusto namin ng ___
We want to ___	GOO-sto NA-meeng ___	Gusto naming ___
Wednesday	M‿YAYR-ko-less	mierkoles
welcome		
You're welcome	wa-LA' poang ah-no-MAHN	Walâ pong anoman
well *(of water)*	ba-LOAN	balon
west	kahn-LOO-rahn	kanluran
what	ah-NO	ano
What's this?	ah-NO ee-TO?	Ano ito?
What time is it?	AH-noang O-rahss na?	Anong oras na?
when	AH-noang O-rahss	anong oras
When does the bus leave?	AH-noang O-rahss ahng ah-LEESS nahng owt-o-BOOSS?	Anong oras ang alis ng autobus?
When does the movie start?	AH-noang O-rahss ahng see-moo-LA' nahng SEE-nay?	Anong oras ang simula ng sine?

English	Pronunciation	Tagalog Spelling
When does the train leave?	AH-noang O-rahss ahng ah-LEESS nahng TREN?	Anong oras ang alis ng tren?
where		
Where can I get ____?	sa-AHN ah-KO ma-ka-ka-KOO-ha nahng ____?	Saan ako makaka-kuha ng ____?
Where is the ____? or Where is a ____?	na-sa-AHN ahng ____?	Nasaan ang ____?
workman	mahng-ga-GA-wa'	manggagawâ
wounded	na-soo-GA-tahn	nasugatan

Y

English	Pronunciation	Tagalog Spelling
Yes	O-po'	opô
yesterday	ka-HA-poan	kahapon
you		
Are you ____?	ee-KOW ba A ee ____?	Ikaw ba ay ____?
Do you want to ____?	GOO-sto ba néen-YOANG ____?	Gusto ba nin-yong ____?
Have you ____?	ma ee-ro-OAN ba ka-YOANG ____?	mayroon ba ka-yong ____?